'What We Have Seen and Heard'

*A Pastoral Letter
on Evangelization
From the Black Bishops
of the United States*

'What We Have Seen and Heard'

A Pastoral Letter on Evangelization From the Black Bishops of the United States

Joseph L. Howze

Harold R. Perry, S.V.D.

Eugene A. Marino, S.S.J.

Joseph A. Francis, S.V.D.

James P. Lyke, O.F.M.

Emerson J. Moore

Moses B. Anderson, S.S.E.

Wilton D. Gregory

J. Terry Steib, S.V.D.

John H. Ricard, S.S.J.

Issued September 9, 1984, Feast of St. Peter Claver

Dedication

To our Holy Father,
Pope John Paul II,
Vicar of Jesus Christ
and Evangelist

Scripture texts used in this work are taken from the *New American Bible*, copyright ©1970, by the Confraternity of Christian Doctrine, Washington, D.C., and are used by permission of the copyright owner. All rights reserved.

Book design by Julie Lonneman.

Cover illustration by Sister Angela Williams, O.S.F.

SBN 0-86716-040-3

©1984, St. Anthony Messenger Press.
All rights reserved.
Printed in the U.S.A.

To Our Black
Catholic Brothers and Sisters
in the United States

*Introduction**

Within the history of every Christian community there comes the time when it reaches adulthood. This maturity brings with it the duty, the privilege and the joy to share with others the rich experience of the "Word of Life." Always conscious of the need to hear the Word and ever ready to listen to its proclamation, the mature Christian community feels the irresistible urge to speak that Word:

> This is what we proclaim to you:
> what was from the beginning,
> what we have heard,
> what we have seen with our eyes,
> what we have looked upon
> and our hands have touched—
> we speak of the word of life.
> (This life became visible;
> we have seen and bear witness to it,
> and we proclaim to you the eternal life
> that was present to the Father
> and became visible to us.)
> What we have seen and heard
> we proclaim in turn to you
> so that you may share life with us.
> This fellowship of ours is with the Father
> and with his son, Jesus Christ.

---

*1, 6-12, 14-16, 17, 20-24, 26-27, 49-58, 75. (*Asterisked citations refer to related paragraphs in Evangelii Nuntiandi.* These citations are not intended to be exhaustive. Numbered citations refer to Endnotes found on p. 37.)

> Indeed, our purpose in writing you this
> is that our joy may be complete. (1 John 1: 1-4)

We, the 10 Black bishops of the United States, chosen from among you to serve the People of God, are a significant sign among many other signs that the Black Catholic community in the American Church has now come of age. We write to you as brothers that "you may share life with us." We write also to all those who by their faith make up the People of God in the United States that "our joy may be complete." And what is this joy? It is that joy that the Ethiopian eunuch, the treasurer of the African queen, expressed in the Book of Acts when he was baptized by the deacon, Philip: He "went on his way rejoicing" (Acts 8:39). We rejoice because, like this African court official, we the descendants of Africans brought to these shores are now called to share our faith and to demonstrate our witness to our risen Lord.

We write to you, Black brothers and sisters, because each one of us is called to a special task. The Holy Spirit now calls us all to the work of evangelization. As he did for Peter, the Lord Jesus has prayed for us that our faith might not fail (Luke 22:32), and with Paul we are all compelled to confess:

> Yet preaching the gospel is not the subject of a boast; I am under compulsion and have no choice. I am ruined if I do not preach it! (1 Corinthians 9:16)

Evangelization is both a call and a response. It is the call of Jesus reverberating down the centuries: "Go into the whole world and proclaim the good news to all creation" (Mark 16:15). The response is: "Conduct yourselves, then, in a way worthy of the gospel of Christ" (Philippians 1:27). Evangelization means not only preaching but witnessing; not only conversion but renewal; not only entry into the community but the building up of the community; not only hearing the Word but sharing it. Evangelization, said Pope Paul VI,

> . . . is a question not only of preaching the Gospel in ever wider geographic areas or to ever greater numbers of people, but also of affecting and as it were upsetting, through the power of the Gospel, mankind's criteria of judgment, determining values, points of interest, lines of thought, sources of inspiration and models of life, which are in contrast

with the Word of God and the plan of Salvation.[1]

Pope Paul VI issued that call to the peoples of Africa when he said to them at Kampala in Uganda: "You are now missionaries to yourselves. . . ." And Pope Paul also laid out for all sons and daughters of Africa the nature of the response: "You must now give your gifts of Blackness to the whole Church."[2]

We believe that these solemn words of our Holy Father Paul VI were addressed not only to Africans today but also to us, the children of the Africans of yesterday. We believe that the Holy Father has laid a challenge before us to share the gift of our Blackness with the Church in the United States. This is a challenge to be evangelizers, and so we want to write about this gift which is also a challenge. First, we shall write about the gifts we share, gifts rooted in our African heritage. Then we wish to write about the obstacles to evangelization that we must still seek to overcome.

Grateful Remembrance for Our Own Evangelization*

Before we go on, however, we must at the beginning remember those who brought us to new birth within the Faith. When we as Black Catholics speak of missionaries, we shall never forget the devoted service that many White priests, vowed religious, and laypersons gave to us as a people and still give to us daily. We shall remember and never forget that this ministry was often given at great personal sacrifice and hardship. The same holds true today.

We remember, especially, that those of us who have grown up in the Faith owe this faith to the Black men and women who have gone before us strong in the Faith and steadfast in their personal conviction. If we have reached adulthood in the fullness of the age of Christ, it is most of all thanks to our fathers and mothers and all our ancestors who kept alive an unflagging commitment to Christ and to his Church throughout the bitter days of slavery and the troubled times of racial segregation. Their faith was passed on to us despite the peculiar structures of racism and bondage that marred the Catholic Church in America in an earlier time.

---

*59, 68-69, 71

Part One

The Gifts We Share

Black Culture and Values: Informed by Faith*

There is a richness in our Black experience that we must share with the entire People of God. These are gifts that are part of an African past. For we have heard with Black ears and we have seen with Black eyes and we have understood with an African heart. We thank God for the gifts of our Catholic faith and we give thanks for the gifts of our Blackness. In all humility we turn to the whole Church that it might share our gifts so that "our joy may be complete."

To be Catholic is to be universal. To be universal is not to be uniform. It does mean, however, that the gifts of individuals and of particular groups become the common heritage shared by all. Just as we lay claim to the gifts of Blackness so we share these gifts within the Black community at large and within the Church. This will be our part in the building up of the whole Church. This will also be our way of enriching ourselves. "For it is in giving that we receive."[3] Finally, it is our way to witness to our brothers and sisters within the Black community that the Catholic Church is both one and also home to us all.

Scripture**

African-American spirituality is based on the Sacred Scriptures. In the dark days of slavery, reading was forbidden, but for our ancestors the Bible was never a closed book. The stories were told and retold in sermons, spirituals and shouts. Proverbs and turns of phrase borrowed freely from the Bible. The Bible was not for our ancestors a mere record of the wonderful works of God in a bygone age; it was a present record of what was soon to come. God will lead his people from

---

*62-64
**42-43

the bondage of Egypt. God will preserve his children in the midst of the fiery furnace. God's power will make the dry bones scattered on the plain snap together, and he will breathe life into them. Above all, the birth and death, the suffering and the sorrow, the burial and the resurrection tell how the story will end for all who are faithful no matter what the present tragedy is.

For Black people the story is our story; the Bible promise is our hope. Thus when the Word of Scripture is proclaimed in the Black community, it is not a new message but a new challenge. Scripture is part of our roots; the Bible has sunk deep into our tradition; and the Good News of the Gospel has been enmeshed in our past of oppression and pain. Still the message was heard and we learned to celebrate in the midst of sorrow, to hope in the depths of despair and to fight for freedom in the face of all obstacles. The time has now come to take this precious heritage and to go and "tell it on the mountain."

Our Gift of Freedom*

The Good News of the Gospel is the message of liberation. "You will know the truth," said Jesus, "and the truth will set you free" (John 8:32). Recently, our Holy Father, Pope John Paul II, spoke at length on the relation between truth and freedom:

> Jesus Himself links "liberation" with knowledge of the truth: "You will know the truth, and the truth will make you free" (Jn. 8:32). In this affirmation is the deep meaning of freedom that Christ gives man, as a consequence coming from knowledge of the truth. It is a question of a spiritual process of maturing, by means of which man becomes a representative and spokesman of "righteousness and holiness" (Eph. 4:24) at the different levels of personal, individual, and social life. But this truth is not mere truth of a scientific or historical nature; it is Christ Himself—the Word incarnate of the Father—who can say of Himself, "I am the way, the truth, the life" (Jn. 14:6). For this reason, Jesus, although aware of what was in store for Him, repeatedly and forcefully, with firmness and with decision, opposed "non-truth" in His earthly life.
>
> This service of truth, participation in the prophetic service of Christ, is a task of the Church, which tries to carry it out in the different historical contexts. It is necessary to call clearly

---

*30-39

by name injustice, the exploitation of man by man, the exploitation of man by the state, or by the mechanisms of systems and regimes. It is necessary to call by name all social injustice, all discrimination, all violence inflicted on man with regard to his body, his spirit, his conscience, his dignity as a person, his life.[4]

Black people know what freedom is because we remember the dehumanizing force of slavery, racist prejudice and oppression. No one can understand so well the meaning of the proclamation that Christ has set us free than those who have experienced the denial of freedom. For us, therefore, freedom is a cherished gift. For its preservation, no sacrifice is too great.

Hence, freedom brings responsibility. It must never be abused, equated with license nor taken for granted. Freedom is God's gift, and we are accountable to him for our loss of it. And we are accountable for the gift of freedom in the lives of others. We oppose all oppression and all injustice, for unless *all* are free, *none* are free. Moreover, oppression by some means freedom's destruction for both the oppressor and the oppressed, and liberation liberates the oppressor and the oppressed.

Our African-American ancestors knew the liberating hand of God. Even before emancipation they knew the inner spiritual freedom that comes from Jesus. Even under slavery they found ways to celebrate that spiritual freedom which God alone can give. They left us the lesson that without spiritual freedom we cannot fight for that broader freedom which is the right of all who are brothers and sisters in Christ. This is the gift we have to share with the whole Church. This is the responsibility that freedom brings: to teach to others its value and work to see that its benefits are denied to none.

The Gift of Reconciliation*

The Gospel message is a message that liberates us from hate and calls us to forgiveness and reconciliation. As a people we must be deeply committed to reconciliation. This is a value coming from our Black heritage and deepened by our belief in the Gospel teaching. When in recent years, we rejected "token integration" for "self-determination," it was not to choose

---

*2, 30-31, 61-64

confrontation in place of cooperation but to insist on collaboration with mutual respect for the dignity and unique gifts of all. Reconciliation can never mean unilateral elevation and another's subordination, unilateral giving and another's constant receiving, unilateral flexibility and another's resistance. True reconciliation arises only where there is mutually perceived equality. This is what is meant by justice.

Without justice, any meaningful reconciliation is impossible. Justice safeguards the rights and delineates the responsibility of all. A people must safeguard their own cultural identity and their own cultural values. Likewise they must respect the cultural values of others. For this reason sincere reconciliation builds on mutual recognition and mutual respect. On this foundation can be erected an authentic Christian love.

> But now in Christ Jesus you who once were far off have been brought near through the blood of Christ. It is he who is our peace, and who made the two of us one by breaking down the barrier of hostility that kept us apart. (Ephesians 2:13-14)

We seek justice, then, because we seek reconciliation, and we seek reconciliation because by the blood of Christ we are made one. The desire for reconciliation is for us a most precious gift, for reconciliation is the fruit of liberation. Our contribution to the building up of the Church in America and in the world is to be an agent of change for both.

Finally, as we speak of reconciliation, let us note that as members of a truly universal Church our efforts must never be limited to the Black community in this country alone. Our minds and hearts turn toward the Church of the Poor in the Third World, especially those "who hunger and thirst for justice" in Africa, Asia and Latin America. We turn also to the members of the Church of Silence and to the various minority groups in the East and in the West.

We shall remind ourselves and our compatriots that we are called to be "instruments of peace." This peace is the fruit of justice. We must be a part of those movements for justice that seek to reduce bombs and increase bread, to replace bullets with the printing of books. We must work with all who strive to make available the fruits of creation to all God's children everywhere. It was in chains that our parents were brought to these shores and in violence were we maintained in bondage.

Let us who are the children of pain be now a bridge of reconciliation. Let us who are the offspring of violence become the channels of compassion. Let us, the sons and daughters of bondage, be the bringers of peace.

Our Spirituality and Its Gifts*

Black Americans are a people rich with spiritual gifts. Some aspects of this spirituality have already been mentioned. It is fitting, however, to present briefly the major characteristics of what can be termed "Black Spirituality." As members of a Church universal both in time and place, we have no difficulty with this term. All peoples and all cultures have been molded by the Holy Spirit, and the Holy Spirit has distributed his gifts in the·language, culture and traditions of each.

Black Spirituality has four major characteristics: It is contemplative. It is holistic. It is joyful. It is communitarian.

The Contemplative Dimension. Black Spirituality is contemplative. By this we mean that prayer is spontaneous and pervasive in the Black tradition. Every place is a place for prayer because God's presence is heard and felt in every place. Black Spirituality senses the awe of God's transcendence and the vital intimacy of his closeness. God's power breaks into the "sin-sick world" of everyday. The sense of God's presence and power taught our ancestors that no one can run from him and no one need hide from him.

Black Spirituality has taught us what it means to "let go" and "to lean on God." In an age of competition and control, we have learned to surrender to God's love and to let him work his power through us. In an age of technology and human engineering, our spiritual heritage has never let us forget that God takes us each by the hand and leads us in ways we might not understand. It is this sense of God's power in us that calls us to work for evangelization in the modern world.

Holistic. Black Spirituality, in contrast with much of Western tradition, is holistic. Like the biblical tradition, there is no dualism. Divisions between intellect and emotion, spirit and body, action and contemplation, individual and community, sacred and secular are foreign to us. In keeping with our African heritage, we are not ashamed of our emotions. For us, the

---

*61-64

religious experience is an experience of the whole human being—both the feelings and the intellect, the heart as well as the head. Moreover, we find foreign any notion that the body is evil. We find our own holistic spiritual approach to be in accord with the Scriptures and the logic of the Incarnation.

In sharing this approach we contribute greatly to evangelization in our day. St. Paul wrote Timothy: "Everything God created is good; nothing is to be rejected when it is received with thanksgiving" (1 Timothy 4:4). The material world need not lead us away from God but can and should bring us closer to him.

We dare to suggest that Black Spirituality in its holistic approach also presents a solution to one of the problems of our time: the progressive dehumanization brought about by a technocratic society. Not only is it possible to counteract the dehumanizing forces in our world and our work but we can restore the human. We can put back the human factor by rediscovering that "the world is charged with the grandeur of God"[5] and that "the whole world is in his hands." We affirm that the advances in technology, when understood with God's presence in all things, will be a powerful force for the coming of the Kingdom and the human progress of all people.

The Gift of Joy. Joy is a hallmark of Black Spirituality. Joy is first of all celebration. Celebration is movement and song, rhythm and feeling, color and sensation, exultation and thanksgiving. We celebrate the presence and the proclamation of the Word.

This joy is a sign of our faith and especially our hope. It is never an escape from reality, however harsh it may be. Indeed this joy is often present even in the midst of deep anguish and bitter tears.

> ". . . you will weep and mourn
> while the world rejoices;
> you will grieve for a time,
> but your grief will be turned into joy." (John 16:20)

This joy is a result of our conviction that "in the time of trouble, he will lead me. . . ." This joy comes from the teaching and wisdom of mothers and fathers in the Faith that, looking at Jesus, we must burst forth into song so that all might hear,

"He's sweet I know. . . ."

This gift of joy is something we must share. If the message of evangelization is the "Good News" about Jesus, we must react with joy. If we do indeed feel a profound joy, we shall know that we have heard and that we have understood; and we are thus enabled to share our Good News.

One who is joyful is impelled to love and cannot hate. A joyful person seeks to reconcile and will not cause division. A joyful person is troubled by the sight of another's sadness. A joyful person seeks to console, strives to encourage and brings to all true peace.

Such is the gift so clearly needed in our time. Such is the gift that Jesus passed on to us on the evening he died.

> "All this I tell you
> that my joy may be yours
> and your joy may be complete." (John 15:11)

*Community.** In African culture the "I" takes its meaning in the "we." In other words, individual identity is to be found within the context of the community. Even today, Black Christianity is eminently a social reality. The sense of community is a major component of Black Spirituality.

This communal dimension of our spirituality is a gift we also need to share. In the world in which we live, a high value is placed on competition. Hence, so many of us become "losers" so that others might prevail as "winners." And again so many place personal profit and personal advancement before the good of the community and the benefit of the whole.

The communal dimension of Black Spirituality permeates our experience of liturgy and worship. Worship must be shared. Worship is always a celebration of community. No one stands in prayer alone. One prays and acts within and for the community. Each one supports, encourages and enriches the other and is in turn enriched, encouraged and supported.

Community, however, means social concern and social justice. Black Spirituality never excludes concern for human suffering and other people's concerns. ". . . As often as you did it for one of my least brothers, you did it for me" (Matthew

---

*60

25:40) are the words of Christ that cut through any supposed tension between secular concerns and the sacred, or between prayerful pursuits and the profane. Ours is a spiritual heritage that always embraces the total human person.

The Family*

The heart of the human community is the family. In our society today, traditional family values are openly questioned and rejected. For many reasons, the Black family has been especially assailed, despite the importance that families still have in the Black cultural and spiritual tradition.

For us the family has always meant "the extended family"—the grandparents, the uncles and aunts, the godparents, all those related by kinship or strong friendship. This rich notion of family was not only part of an African tradition but also was our own African-American experience. Child care became the responsibility of many persons, for necessity demanded that many share the labor, distribute the burden and, yes, even the joy.

In practice, the extended family often goes beyond kinship and marital relationship to include persons who, having no family of their own, have been accepted into the wider family circle. These family members feel a deep responsibility for one another in both ordinary times of daily life and in the extraordinary moments of need or crisis.

It is for this reason that, despite the erosion of family life among us, we as a people continue to have a strong sense of family bonds. In its Christian setting, this family sense enhances the role of godparents and other relatives who must often shoulder the responsibility for passing on the Faith and strengthening the religious values of the young. Moreover, there is more than one priestly or religious vocation among us that was nurtured by the support and encouragement of some adult in the extended family. Not infrequently young Blacks in the seminary or religious formation house have been informally adopted by a sponsor or have been welcomed into the circle of a second family.

This sense of family in our own African-American tradition can easily be translated into a richer sense of Church as

---

*71

a great and all-embracing family. In our parishes we should truly look upon ourselves as brothers and sisters to one another. The elders among us should be a living resource for the young, for they have much to tell and teach. Our celebrations should be the affirmation of our kinship and our common bond. The words of the third Eucharistic Prayer, "Father, hear the prayers of the family you have gathered here before you," are not a pious fiction but a sacred reality that defines the meaning of the Catholic community. In a word, evangelization for Black Catholics is a celebration of the family, a renewal of the family, and a call to welcome new members into the Family of God.

*The Role of Black Men.** Central to any discussion of the Black family today is the question of the Black man as husband, father, co-provider and co-protector. For many historical reasons, the Black man has been forced to bear the crushing blows of racial hate and economic repression. Too often barred from access to decent employment, too often stripped of his dignity and manhood, and too often forced into a stereotype that was a caricature of his manhood, the Black male finds himself depreciated and relegated to the margins of family life and influence. Not the least of the evil fruits of racial segregation has been the artificially fashioned rivalry between Black women and men.

It is important, we believe, to encourage a reevaluation of the fundamental vocation to fatherhood that Black men must have in the context of the Black family. In our cultural heritage, the father provides the courage and wisdom to help maintain the family and to insure its growth. We challenge Black men of today to assert their spiritual strength and to demonstrate their sense of responsibility and ethnic pride. We call upon Black men to become what their fathers were—even when an evil institution sought to destroy their individuality and their initiative—that is, models of virtue for their children and partners in love and nurturing with their wives. Without a father no family life can be fully complete. Let the Black father find his model in the Fatherhood of God, who by his providence nourishes us, who by his wisdom guides us, and who by his love cherishes us and makes us all one and holy in his family of grace.

*73, 76

*The Role of Women.** The Civil Rights Movement of the 1960's that we as a people initiated and in which we suffered raised the consciousness of many people to the reality of social inequities and social injustice. In many ways our struggle served as a pattern and a model for others who were made aware of their own plight. Within the last decade we all have become more conscious of the social inequities that women as a group have suffered and continue to suffer in our society. In a very special way these inequities weigh most heavily on Black women and women of other racial minorities.

On the other hand, Black women have had and continue to have a place within the Black community that is unique. In traditional Black society women have had to assume responsibilities within the family and within the community out of necessity. As a result, Black women historically have been not only sources of strength, but they also have been examples of courage and resolution. This strength and courage is for us all a source of power and a powerful gift that we as a people can share with the larger society.

The role of Black women within the context of Black history, however, has not been a subordinate role to Black men but a complementary role. Women like Sojourner Truth, Harriet Tubman and Mary McLeod Bethune were heirs of a Black tradition.

If this is true of the African-American tradition, it is even more so for us who are the heirs of a Black Catholic tradition. Before there were Black Catholic priests in the United States, there were Black women religious. The challenge of evangelization within the Black Catholic community was taken up by four Black women in the hostile environment of Baltimore under the leadership of Elizabeth Lange. The Church gave approval to her work when the Oblate Sisters of Providence were officially recognized as a religious congregation in 1831. Evangelization among the Blacks of New Orleans was also the task assumed by Henriette Delille, who in the face of crushing opposition founded the Sisters of the Holy Family in 1842. These two Black congregations of religious women were joined by a third in our own century when Mother Theodore Williams helped establish the Franciscan Handmaids of the Most Pure

---

*73, 76

13

Heart of Mary in 1916 in Savannah, Georgia.

These Black women religious leaders and the sisters whom they formed were not only witnesses of Faith; they were also a sign of the Faith of many Black Catholic families who even in the dark days of slavery gave not only support but even their daughters and sisters in the service of the Gospel.

Within the Black Catholic community today, Black women continue to witness in various non-ordained ministries, both as religious and lay. This ministry is to be found on the parochial and the diocesan level. It is a ministry in schools and in the social apostolate. Needless to say, this potential for service within our own community needs to be more fully recognized and utilized by the Catholic Church in the United States. Black women can and should be considered as collaborators in the work of evangelization. The words of the Pastoral Commission of the Congregation for the Propagation of the Faith are eminently true of women in the Black Catholic community:

> Givers of life, consecrated by nature to its service, it is for women to give to evangelization a living and realistic face before the world.[6]

*Abortion and Black Values.** Today the Black family is assailed on all sides. Much has been said by others about the economic plight of the Black family. We would like to add a word regarding the moral aspect of this plight.

The acceptance of abortion by many as a common procedure and even as a right is a reality not only in our American society as a whole, but also within the Black community. And yet life, and especially new life within the mother, has always been a value to Africans and to African Americans. Historically, even children conceived outside of marriage were cherished and given a place in the extended family. Black cultural tradition has always valued life and the mystery of its transmission and growth. Children have always been for us a sign of hope. The loss of this perspective is a cultural and spiritual impoverishment for us as a people.

From our point of view as Catholics and as Black people,

---

*65

we see the efforts made "to provide" low-cost abortions as another form of subjugation. Indeed there are those who would even characterize it as a form of genocide. As a people of faith, it is our task to fight for the right to life of all our children and in all the circumstances of their existence. It is our duty to reassert the gift of our traditional African-American values of family and children to our own people and to our society as a whole. It is equally our duty, however, to show practical concern and honest compassion for the many mothers-to-be who are too often encouraged to seek an abortion by the conventional wisdom of our society today.

Finally, we add this unfortunate observation: If society truly valued our children and our mothers—mothers who have already made a choice for life—they would have day care centers, jobs, good schools and all else that a just society should offer to its people. Sadly, we observe that if abortion were abolished tomorrow, the same disastrous ills would plague our Black mothers and children.

Ecumenism*

There exists a reality which is called "The Black Church." It crosses denominational boundaries and is without a formal structure. Yet it is a reality cherished by many Black Christians, who feel at ease joining in prayer and in Christian action with one another. This Black Church is a result of our common experience and history—it has made it possible for many Blacks to understand and appreciate each other.

This does not mean that Black people, and especially Black Catholics, are indifferent to the distinctions of various denominations. Black Catholics as well as all Black Christians are loyal to their respective faith communities. Black Catholics most particularly, whether by birth or conversion in later life, insist upon total loyalty to all that is Catholic. A deep abiding love of the Catholic Church is a characteristic of Black Catholicism.

Nevertheless, because we as a people have been a deeply religious people, we as Black Catholics are in a special position to serve as a bridge with our brothers and sisters of other Christian traditions. We wish to encourage our Black

---

*39, 65-68, 77-79, 80

Catholics to deepen their awareness and understanding of the whole Black Church, inasmuch as the majority of Black Christians in this country are separated from Catholic unity.

It is to this end that Pope Paul VI called us when he stated:

> As Catholics our best ecumenical efforts are directed both to removing the causes of separation that still remain, as well as to giving adequate expression to the communion which already exists among all Christians. We are sustained and encouraged in this task because so many of the most significant elements and endowments "that are Christ's gift to his Church are the common source of our strength."[7]

And, in reference to the wealth of spiritual joy and expression in the Black Church, these words spoken by Pope John Paul II in New York would seem especially appropriate for us:

> . . . I wish to greet in you the rich variety of your nation, where people of different ethnic origins and creeds can live, work and prosper together in mutual respect.[8]

Finally, the following words of Pope John Paul II would seem appropriate for our relationships with our Muslim and Jewish brothers and sisters:

> Does it not sometimes happen that the firm belief of the followers of the non-Christian religions—a belief that is also an effect of the Spirit of truth operating outside the visible confines of the mystical body—can make Christians ashamed at being often themselves so disposed to doubt concerning the truths revealed by God and proclaimed by the Church and so prone to relax moral principles and open the way to ethical permissiveness.[9]

Part Two

The Call of God to His People

*Perspective**

If the story of America is told with honesty and clarity, we must all recognize the role that Blacks have played in the growth of this country. At every turning point of American history, we come face to face with the Black man and Black woman. What is true of our national history is even truer of American Catholic history.

Just as the Church in our history was planted by the efforts of the Spaniards, the French and the English, so did she take root among Indians, Black slaves and the various racial mixtures of them all. Blacks—whether Spanish-speaking, French-speaking or English-speaking—built the churches, tilled Church lands, and labored with those who labored in spreading the Gospel. From the earliest period of the Church's history in our land, we have been the hands and arms that helped build the Church from Baltimore to Bardstown, from New Orleans to Los Angeles, from St. Augustine to St. Louis. Too often neglected and too much betrayed, our faith was witnessed by Black voices and Black tongues—such as Jean-Baptiste Pointe du Sable, Pierre Toussaint, Elizabeth Lange, Henriette Delille and Augustus Tolton.

The historical roots of Black America and those of Catholic America are intimately intertwined. Now is the time for us who are Black Americans and Black Catholics to reclaim our roots and to shoulder the responsibilities of being both Black and Catholic.

The responsibility is both to our own people and to our own Church. To the former, we owe the witness of our Faith in Christ and in his Body, the Church. To the latter, we owe this witness of faith as well as the unstinting labor to denounce

---

*61-62

racism as a sin and to work for justice and inner renewal.

It is to this responsibility that we now address ourselves in this second half of our pastoral letter. We do so by setting forth the opportunities and challenges that lie before us as a people and as a Church.

Black Initiative*

We call upon our Black Catholic sisters and brothers to shoulder the responsibility laid upon us by our Baptism into the Body of Christ. This responsibility is to proclaim our faith and to take an active part in building up the Church. The Second Vatican Council in its *Decree on the Missionary Activity of the Church* stated:

> The Church has not been truly established and is not yet fully alive, nor is it a perfect sign of Christ among men, unless there exists a laity worthy of the name working along with the hierarchy. . . .
> Their main duty . . . is the witness which they are bound to bear to Christ by their life and works in the home, in their social group, and in their own professional circle. . . . They must give expression to this newness of life in the social and cultural framework of their own homeland, according to their own national traditions. They must heal it and preserve it. . . . Let them also spread the faith of Christ among those with whom they live. . . . This obligation is all the more urgent, because very many men can hear of the gospel and recognize Christ only by means of the laity who are their neighbors. . . .[10]

The Black community in the United States for a long time has been a component of the missionary enterprise of the American Church. In this sense these words from the *Decree on Missionary Activity* are perfectly valid for the American Black community. We are conscious of the debt of gratitude we owe to those who have served among us as home missionaries.

Yet we are also aware that we, like other African Americans, are also descendants of slaves and freedmen. Like them we are victims of oppression and racism, and like them we are fighters for the same freedom and dignity. We likewise speak with the same accents and sing the same songs, and we

---

*62-63

are heirs of the same cultural achievements. Thus we have a privileged position to gain access to the hearts and minds of the African-American community. Hence, we now have the solemn responsibility to take the lead in the Church's work within the Black community.

On the other hand, we are in a position to counter the assumption which many have advanced that to become a Catholic is to abandon one's racial heritage and one's people! The Catholic Church is not a "White Church" nor a "Euro-American Church." It is essentially universal and, hence, Catholic. The Black presence within the American Catholic Church is a precious witness to the universal character of Catholicism.

The Church, however, must preserve its multi-cultural identity. As Paul VI wrote:

> Evangelization loses much of its force and effectiveness if it does not take into consideration the actual people to whom it is addressed, if it does not use their language, their signs and symbols, if it does not answer the questions they ask, and if it does not have an impact on their concrete life. . . .[11]

In our response to the invitation to evangelize, we as Black Catholics have before us several opportunities to assure the universal aspect of the American Church. We can do so by permitting the Catholic Church in this country to reflect the richness of African-American history and its heritage. This is our gift to the Church in the United States, this is our contribution to the building up of the Universal Church.

Authorization and Encouragement*

Since African-American members of the American Church are to assume the responsibility to which the Church and our racial heritage call us, Black leaders in the Church—clergy, religious and lay—need encouragement and the authorization to use their competencies and to develop their expertise. Unhappily, we must acknowledge that the major hindrance to the full development of Black leadership within the Church is still the fact of racism. The American Catholic bishops wrote in the pastoral letter on racism:

---

*66-73

> The Church . . . must be constantly attentive to the Lord's voice as he calls on his people daily not to harden their hearts (Psalm 94:8). We urge that on all levels the Catholic Church in the United States examine its conscience regarding attitudes and behavior toward Blacks, Hispanics, Native Americans and Asians. We urge consideration of the evil of racism as it exists in the local Church and reflection upon the means of combating it. We urge scrupulous attention at every level to insure that minority representation goes beyond mere tokenism and involves authentic sharing in the responsibility and decision-making.[12]

These words have not had the full impact on the American Church that was originally hoped. Blacks and other minorities still remain absent from many aspects of Catholic life and are only meagerly represented on the decision-making level. Inner-city schools continue to disappear and Black vocational recruitment lacks sufficient support. In spite of the fact that Catholic schools are a principal instrument of evangelization, active evangelization is not always a high priority.

This racism, at once subtle and masked, still festers within our Church as within our society. It is this racism that in our minds remains the major impediment to evangelization within our community. Some little progress has been made, but success is not yet attained. This stain of racism on the American Church continues to be a source of pain and disappointment to all, both Black and White, who love her and desire her to be the Bride of Christ "without stain or wrinkle" (Ephesians 5:27). This stain of racism, which is so alien to the Spirit of Christ, is a scandal to many, but for us it must be the opportunity to work for the Church's renewal as part of our task of evangelization. To "profess the truth in love" (Ephesians 4:15) to our brothers and sisters within the Faith remains for Black Catholics the first step in proclaiming the Gospel message. We, like St. John the Baptist, proclaim a baptism of repentence for the forgiveness of sins, and we call on the American Church to produce the fruit of repentance and not presume to tell themselves we have Abraham for our father, for we all belong to the Family of God (cf. Luke 3:1-9).

Our demand for recognition, our demand for leadership roles in the task of evangelization, is not a call for separatism but a pledge of our commitment to the Church and to share in her witnessing to the love of Christ. For the Christ we proclaim is he who prayed on the night before he died

> ". . . that all may be one
> as you, Father, are in me, and I in you;
> I pray that they may be [one] in us,
> that the world may believe that you sent me." (John 17:21)

Opportunities for Evangelization

There exist numerous opportunities for evangelization within the Black community. It is not our intention to enumerate all of these. We do propose, however, to point out those that in our opinion are the most important and the most essential. For some of these the Black community can and must seize the initiative. For others we need the cooperation and the encouragement of the entire American Church.

Vocations to the Priesthood and to the Religious Life. From apostolic times, the local Church called forth its ministers from within itself for the sake of evangelization. Paul and Barnabas evangelized the communities of Iconium, Lystra and Derbe. "In each church they installed presbyters and, with prayer and fasting, commended them to the Lord in whom they had put their faith" (Acts 14:23). This became the established practice: to plant the new Church and draw from it the clergy and the teachers to continue the work of evangelization and nurture the growing congregation with pastoral care. In this way were the early Churches of Africa evangelized in Egypt, Nubia, Ethiopia and North Africa.

Unfortunately, later missionaries did not always carry out this traditional practice. For too long, the way to a fully indigenous clergy and religious was blocked by an attitude that was paternalistic and racist. It was especially through the efforts of the Holy See that the earlier practice was resumed. Beginning with Pope Benedict XV in 1919 with the encyclical *Maximum Illud*, and continuing on until the Second Vatican Council, the highest authority within the Church has called in season and out of season for the creation of an indigenous clergy. This was to be done as soon as possible as part of the actual process of evangelization:

> . . . it is not enough for the Christian people to be present and organized in a given nation. Nor is it enough for them to carry

21

> out an apostolate of good example. They are organized and present for the purpose of announcing Christ to their non-Christian fellow-citizens by word and deed, and of aiding them toward the full reception of Christ.
>
> Now, if the Church is to be planted and the Christian community grow, various ministries are needed. These are raised up by divine vocation from the midst of the faithful, and are to be carefully fostered and cultivated by all.[13]

If in the history of the American Church many Black men and women found their vocations to the religious life and priesthood blocked by racist attitudes, this is no longer tolerable. It is now the responsibility and the duty of the Black Catholic community to encourage young men and women to follow Christ in the priesthood and in the consecrated life.

The duty lies especially with all those who have contact with youth. We call first upon the Black family to set before the eyes of the young the value of service to Christ in ministry of others, both at the altar and in the manifold areas of evangelization. Black parents will do this by passing on to their children the truths of the Catholic religion and the spiritual values of our African-American heritage. When a child shows signs of a priestly or religious vocation, the parents will respect and even encourage this sign of God's call.

We call upon teachers and educators and all those who work with youth in the Black community to be aware of this vocation when it appears among Black youth. Let them not underestimate their influence for good regarding the young. Let them never belittle or discourage the manifestation of the Spirit. Moreover, let them encourage those more mature men and women who, touched by grace, follow a religious vocation as a second career.

Most particularly we remind our Black sisters and brothers who have already answered God's call that they especially have the task to foster Black vocations. All young people crave role models. Black sisters, brothers and priests must be such models for Black youth today. Let them take care to be always a positive influence. If in their own lives of service they have had to struggle because of racial discrimination, let them now be beacons of hope for those who follow after. Even if in their own lives they have experienced the contradictions of a racist society, let them show forth the joy that comes to those who leave all to follow the crucified King.

In this matter of vocations, so crucial to the cause of evangelization in the Black community, we need the collaboration of the entire American Church. In fact, we suggest that the recruitment of minority youth for the priesthood and religious life must have the highest priority. More precisely, let diocesan vocation directors collaborate with leaders in the Black Catholic community in strategic planning for the recruitment of Black young men for the diocesan priesthood. The same planning and collaborative effort should be part of the vocational planning of the many religious congregations and seminaries. Care should be taken to know and understand the attitudes and concerns of Black young people in order to show how ministry would be relevant to their lives and experience. Above all, it is necessary for those engaged in recruitment programs, whether for the diocesan clergy or for religious life, to go where Black young people are found. It means visits to inner-city schools and the use of vocational materials that portray Blacks, Hispanics, Asians and other racial or ethnic groups.

Regretfully, experience has shown that once inside a seminary, a novitiate or a house of formation many minority students face a period of cultural and social alienation. Here again, collaborative effort is needed between seminary and formation leaders on the one hand, and the minority community on the other. In the case of Black students this means helping the student to maintain contact with the Black community and to renew contact with Black culture, Black history and Black theological studies. The National Conference of Catholic Bishops called for this in 1981:

> . . . students who come from diverse racial and cultural backgrounds should participate in programs and adopt a pattern of life geared to ready them for pastoral responsibility among their respective peoples and to intensify their own sense of ethnic identity. . . .
> Seminarians from various ethnic groups need to maintain and develop their identity with both family and community. This will require special sensitivity on the part of those responsible for administration and formation.[14]

Not only Blacks but all who would work in and with the Black community must understand the history, values, culture and ethos of the Black community. The American bishops call for this in the same document.

> The seminary should include in its program of studies courses presenting the history and the development of the cultural heritage of black, Hispanic, and native Americans, and other cultural and ethnic groups within the United States. Moreover, opportunities for intercultural contacts should be offered, to enable future ministers to become more aware, through workshops, seminars, and special sessions, of the positive values offered by other cultures. . . . Such an experience is imperative for those whose ministry, because of the ethnic population of their region, will bring them into contact with large numbers of certain racial and cultural groups. . . .
>
> The seminary course in Church history should also include a treatment of the Church's relationship to these various ethnic groups, to give an insight into present difficulties facing the Church in her ministry to minority groups in the United States today.[15]

Finally, we believe it important that Black men and women be encouraged to follow the Spirit in every sector of the Church. This will include the strictly contemplative orders as well. It is our profound conviction that the Holy Spirit is working among us as a people and will continue to work to bring forth fruits of holiness and prayer.

Permanent Deacons. It is a sign of the times that the Second Vatican Council in its wisdom called for the restoration of the permanent order of deacons. In the Black community this unique calling is of special importance because it provides an opportunity for men of competence who have had an experience of life much broader than that of many priests and religious. Even after ordination, many permanent deacons continue to pursue their occupation in the workaday world and in family life. This gives them access to opportunities for evangelization in places where a priest or religious might find entry difficult. This is particularly true for Black deacons in the Black community where many of the clergy are not Black. The permanent diaconate provides an opportunity to utilize those men who are natural leaders. Furthermore, it makes use of an institution that is familiar to most Blacks, since deacons are part of the congregation in many Black Christian communities.

The permanent diaconate sacramentalizes this reality which is already present, and gives it a prestige which cannot but redound to the advantage of the Church in proclaiming the Good News to the whole community. Incorporated into the hierarchy through the Sacrament of Orders and yet part of the community in whose life he shares, the Black deacon has a role of mediator which is truly unique.

Every effort should be made to recruit qualified candidates for the Office of Deacon from within every Black parish. All members of the parish community should be involved. Pastors should actively strive to identify and recruit likely candidates. Those who feel the desire to serve in this way should prayerfully and assiduously pursue their call. All members of the parish can make an invaluable contribution by searching out candidates and giving them encouragement and support.

What we have said regarding the formation of Black priests and religious applies to that of deacons as well. If anything, it is even more important. The deacon is called for service not only in the parish but also at times in the diocese at large. This service demands the acquisition of those skills necessary for effective ministry. The Black deacon especially must synthesize in his life and in his understanding not only faith but also his cultural and racial heritage. We call upon those responsible for the deacon's training and formation to prepare him for this unique task.

*The Laity.** The work of evangelization is not confined to the clergy and the religious alone. It is also the responsibility of the laity.

> Incorporated into Christ's Mystical Body through baptism and strengthened by the power of the Holy Spirit through confirmation, they are assigned to the apostolate by the Lord himself.[16]

Within the tradition of the Black community, laypersons in the Black Church have always had important roles. Within the history of the Black Catholic community, at a time when the Black clergy were few, many laypersons provided leadership. We need only mention Daniel Rudd and the Black Lay Catholic Congresses in the 19th century, and Thomas Wyatt Turner and

---

*24, 38, 41, 54

The Federated Colored Catholics in the period prior to the Second World War.

The role of the laity needs to be better understood by both the clergy and the laity themselves. In many instances this will require study and reflection, and in some cases a change in attitude. Such understanding, moreover, is only a beginning; for if the laity are to exercise their special form of evangelization, that which is understood in theory must lead to practical plans for action and even structural change.

It is the responsibility of the clergy to facilitate, inspire and coordinate the work of the whole Christian community. This entails calling upon lay women and lay men to join in the work of spreading the Good News, and authorizing and encouraging them to do so. It also means involving them in the formulation and execution of all programs leading to the building up of the Body of Christ, which is the Church.

Lay people in turn must become more aware of their responsibilities and their opportunities for furthering the mission of the Church. They must not passively wait for directives or even an invitation from the clergy. As the Second Vatican Council has pointed out:

> Certain forms of the apostolate of the laity are given explicit recognition by the hierarchy, though in various ways. . . .
> Thus, making various dispositions of the apostolate according to circumstances, the hierarchy joins some particular form of it more closely with its own apostolic function. Yet the proper nature and individuality of each apostolate must be preserved, and the laity must not be deprived of the possibility of acting on their own accord.[17]

Adulthood in Christ, to which all the laity are called, means seizing the opportunity for initiative and creativity in place of complaining about what cannot be done.

Above all let there be no strife or conflict among us as a community and a people. How important it is to recognize and to respect each other's gifts! The pressures of the present age and the pressures of a minority status inevitably lead at times to self-doubt and even self-disdain. But there is always the love of Christ which calls us beyond ourselves and even beyond our local concerns and rivalries.

Each of us has received God's favor in the measure in which Christ bestows it. . . . It is he who gave apostles, prophets, evangelists, pastors and teachers in roles of service for the faithful to build up the body of Christ, till we become one in the faith and in the knowledge of God's Son, and form that perfect man who is Christ come to full stature.

(Ephesians 4:7,11-13)

Youth.* Our youth are the present and the future of the Church in the Black community. If they must be the subject of evangelization in a special way, they should also be taught that they too have a unique opportunity to evangelize their peers.

Black youth are especially vulnerable in our modern society. Today's youth in the Black community undergo many pressures. Especially in our urban areas—where disillusionment and despair, desires and drugs, passion and poverty entrap the young—adults and mature youths dedicated to Christ are needed to counsel, to inspire and to motivate those whom Jesus loved and placed first in his Kingdom. These youths in turn will be the heralds of the Kingdom to other young people in our urban areas today.

Programs for youth—such as retreats, camps, recreational facilities, youth centers and vacation schools—need to be tailored for the Black community following the guidelines for youth ministry set up by the local Church. Black Catholics who commit themselves to a vigorous youth ministry are to be commended and supported on the parish and diocesan level.

The Rite of Christian Initiation of Adults.** The newly restored *Rite of Christian Initiation of Adults*, creatively adapted to the life and culture of the Black community, will serve as a powerful instrument of evangelization among our people. The careful and thorough preparation of the catechumens; the appeal to the whole person, both head and heart (so characteristic of Black Spirituality); the graduated liturgical stages of involvement by the whole Christian community—all these are features of the new Rite which recommend it to us as especially useful for the work of evangelization.

We strongly urge that those among us competent to do so undertake as soon as possible the study needed to adapt the

---

*72
**17-18, 23, 47

Rite to the Black situation. We appeal to the appropriate
authorities of the Church to encourage this endeavor.

*Catholic Education.** Even prior to emancipation, Blacks
in the United States clamored for educational opportunities.
Families uprooted themselves, necessities were sacrificed, extra
toil was assumed in order that the children would receive an
education and, where possible, an even better one was expected
for each succeeding child. Today many parents, very often
single parents, make similar sacrifices; for Black people believe
that the key to a better life is the school.

Black Catholics have placed their hope in Catholic
schools with even greater zeal. The first Black Lay Catholic
Congress in 1889 wrote:

> The education of a people being the great and fundamental
> means of elevating it to the higher planes to which all Christian
> civilization tends, we pledge ourselves to aid in establishing,
> wherever we are to be found, Catholic schools, embracing the
> primary and higher branches of knowledge, as in them and
> through them alone can we expect to reach the large masses of
> Colored children now growing up in this country without a
> semblance of Christian education.[18]

Today the Catholic school still represents for many in
the Black community, especially in the urban areas, an
opportunity for quality education and character development. It
also represents—and this is no less important—a sign of stability
in an environment of chaos and flux. It should be a source of
legitimate pride that our schools are sought after by many who
are not Catholic as well as Catholics because of the religious and
moral values considered as part of a quality education.

The Catholic school has been and remains one of the
chief vehicles of evangelization within the Black community.
We cannot overemphasize the tremendous importance of
parochial schools for the Black community. We even dare to
suggest that the efforts made to support them and to insure
their continuation are a touchstone of the local Church's sincerity
in the evangelization of the Black community.

We are aware of the economic reality, but we are equally
aware of the Gospel injunction to teach all peoples (cf. Matthew

---

*40

28:19). Cost effectiveness can never be the sole criterion for decisions regarding the continuation of a Catholic school in the Black community. For this reason we express our profound admiration and deep gratitude to our fellow bishops, religious communities and laypersons, along with other Church leaders who with a true evangelical spirit have done so much to maintain Catholic schools in our neighborhoods. We remind those who must make decisions concerning these schools to consult with the people of the community, inviting them to participate during the entire process when any decision concerning the existence of a particular school is to be made.

On the other hand, Catholic schools in our neighborhoods should be the concern of the entire Black community. As an important agent for evangelization they must be the concern even of those who have no children in the schools. By the same token, these schools must be thoroughly Catholic in identity and teaching. This does not mean coercing students to join the Catholic Church, but rather to expose all the students to the religious values and teaching that make these schools unique. In a particular way this means that faculty, administration, staff and students will by their manner of life bear witness to Gospel values. In this way not a few—as experience has shown—will freely choose to investigate the Catholic Faith and seek fellowship within the Catholic community.

Support should also be given to Catholic and public institutions of higher learning as well as the traditional Black colleges which have particularly close ties with the Black community. Their excellence in scholarship and their continued growth should be a constant concern for Black Catholics. Xavier University in New Orleans, the only Black Catholic university in the United States, should hold a pride of place for us. Similarly, Newman Centers on public campuses, which have the means of addressing the spiritual needs of our people, deserve our special attention.

Finally, we address an invitation to Black youth and Black adults to consider well the profession of teaching on all levels of Catholic education in our community. Theirs is a wonderful opportunity to spread the Kingdom in the Black community.

When a man is wise to his own advantage,
 the fruits of his knowledge are seen in his own person;
When a man is wise to his people's advantage,
 the fruits of his knowledge are enduring. (Sirach 37:21-22)

*Liturgy.** The celebration of the Sacred Mysteries is that moment when the Church is most fully actualized and most clearly revealed. No treatment of evangelization would be complete without a discussion of the role of liturgy in this regard.

In the African-American tradition the communal experience of worship has always had a central position. In our heritage the moment of celebration has always been a time for praise and thanksgiving, and the affirmation of ourselves as God's children. It is a moment of profound expression, not a flight from reality (as some have suggested), but an experience of God's power and love.

From the standpoint of evangelization in the Black community, the liturgy of the Catholic Church has always demonstrated a way of drawing many to the Faith and also of nourishing and deepening the faith of those who already believe. We believe that the liturgy of the Catholic Church can be an even more intense expression of the spiritual vitality of those who are of African origin, just as it has been for other ethnic and cultural groups:

> . . . the Church has no wish to impose a rigid uniformity in matters which do not involve the faith or the good of the whole community. Rather she respects and fosters the spiritual adornments and gifts of the various races and peoples.[19]

Through the liturgy, Black people will come to realize that the Catholic Church is a homeland for Black believers just as she is for people of other cultural and ethnic traditions. In recent years, remarkable progress has been made in our country by many talented Black experts to adapt the liturgy to the needs and the genius of the African-American community. In order that this work can be carried on more fully within the Catholic tradition and at the same time be enriched by our own cultural

---

*17, 23, 42-43, 47

heritage, we wish to recall the essential qualities that should be found in a liturgical celebration within the Black Catholic community. It should be authentically Black. It should be truly Catholic. And it should be well prepared and well executed.

Authentically Black. The liturgy is simultaneously a ritualization of the divine reality which transcends all human limitations and also an expression of what is most intimate and personal in the participants. What is expressed is the Mystery of Christ which transcends all cultures. The way, however, in which this Mystery is expressed is mediated by the culture and traditions of the participants. All people should be able to recognize themselves when Christ is presented, and all should be able to experience their own fulfillment when these mysteries are celebrated. Hence, we can legitimately speak of an African-American cultural idiom or style in music, in preaching, in bodily expression, in artistic furnishings and vestments, and even in tempo. It is for this reason that we encourage those in pastoral ministry to introduce the African-American idiom into the expression of the Roman liturgy.

It is not our purpose at this time to detail all the characteristics this African-American cultural idiom may have, nor to suggest the limits of cultural authenticity. It is important that from our own community there arise competent liturgical scholars and artists who will mutually contribute to a Black Catholic liturgical critique.

We do wish to remind our fellow Black Catholics, however, that the African-American cultural heritage is vast and rich. The cultural idiom of American Black people has never been uniform but has varied according to region and ethos. African, Haitian, Latin and West Indian cultural expressions also continue to this day to nurture the Black American cultural expression. For this reason, an authentic Black Catholic liturgy need never be confined to a narrowly based concept of what is truly Black. There is a spendid opportunity for the vast richness of African-American culture to be expressed in our liturgy. It is this opportunity, thanks to the norms established in the revised Roman liturgy, which enables our work of evangelization to be filled with such promise for the future.

Truly Catholic. The liturgy not only expresses the worship of a given Catholic community, it also expresses the unity of the Catholic Church. Black Catholic liturgy should express not only our African-American cultural heritage but also our Catholic Faith and unity. In this way, unlike some other Christian communities in the Black community, our worship is not confined to preaching the Word alone, but also includes the Sacrament as celebration.

For this reason neither the preaching nor the music nor any other ritual action have exclusive domain at liturgical celebration. If one or the other prevails, the evangelical dimension as well as the prayerful experience of the liturgy suffers.

> Evangelization thus exercises its full capacity when it achieves the most intimate relationship, or better still, a permanent and unbroken intercommunication, between the Word and the Sacraments. In a certain sense it is a mistake to make a contrast between evangelization and sacramentalization. . . . The role of evangelization is precisely to educate people in the faith in such a way as to lead each individual Christian to live the sacraments as true sacraments of faith—and not to receive them passively or reluctantly.[20]

Both the liturgical preaching and the music should invite the worshiping community to a more profound participation in the total sacramental experience. Neither preaching nor music should overwhelm the liturgical worship and prevent it from exhibiting a balanced unified action.

Proper Preparation and Excellence in Execution. We wish to commend those who have tirelessly presented workshops and conferences on Black liturgical expression. We urge the continued training of liturgists and musicians from the Black Catholic community. We likewise wish to commend those who have generously given their talents as musicians and artists for the enhancement of our liturgical worship. We wish to encourage Black artists, composers, musicians and vocalists to continue to dedicate their skills in God's service. Finally, we urge men and women steeped in the African-American tradition and culture to collaborate with our liturgical scholars in the development of liturgical worship in our community. It is especially in this regard that we can use our rich gifts of Blackness for the whole Church.

In the liturgy, preparation begins with prayerful reflection and is completed and perfected by an execution that culminates in total prayer. We urge that this prayerful preparation and prayerful performance and execution be the result of a collaborative effort of many gifted people each Sunday in our parishes.

*The Social Apostolate.** The proclamation of the Good News by Jesus began with the proclamation of justice and compassion in the context of social reform:

> When the book of the prophet Isaiah was handed him, he unrolled the scroll and found the passage where it was written:
>
>> "The spirit of the Lord is upon me;
>>   therefore he has anointed me.
>> He has sent me to bring glad tidings to the poor,
>>   to proclaim liberty to captives,
>> Recovery of sight to the blind
>>   and release to prisoners,
>> To announce a year of favor from the Lord." (Luke 4:17-19)

For us the causes of justice and social concern are an essential part of evangelization. Our own history has taught us that preaching to the poor and to those who suffer injustice without concern for their plight and the systemic cause of their plight is to trivialize the Gospel and mock the cross. To preach to the powerful without denouncing oppression is to promise Easter without Calvary, forgiveness without conversion, and healing without cleansing the wound.

Our concern for social justice, moreover, goes beyond denouncing injustice in the world around us. It brings us to the examination of our own hearts and intentions. It reminds us that it was the despised and rejected Samaritan who had the compassion to bind up the wounds of the other and to provide a lesson for the Chosen (cf. Luke 10:29-37). As Black people in a powerful nation we must have concern for those who hunger and thirst for justice everywhere in the present world. We must not forget that in a world of suffering even compassion may still be selective. Let us not ignore those whom others tend to forget. It should be our concern to remind others of the plight of Haitian refugees, the hunger of drought-ridden Africans, the forgotten Blacks in a war-torn Namibia, and the many other

---

*8-12, 29-39

forgotten minorities and ill-starred majorities in the world of the downtrodden and deprived. Political expediency and diplomatic advantages should not be bought with the human rights of others.

As a people we must have the courage to speak out and even contribute our efforts and money on behalf of any people or any segment of the human family that the powerful may seek to neglect or forget as a matter of policy. Be assured that we too must render an account for what the Lord has given us (cf. Psalm 116:12). When we share our talents and our possessions with the forgotten ones of this world, we share Christ. This is not the prelude to evangelization, it is the essence of evangelization itself.

Conclusion*

We write this letter to you, our brothers and sisters, strong in the faith and in the knowledge that what has been begun in you will be brought to perfection in the Day of our Lord Jesus Christ. We urge you to study and discuss the points laid before you in this, our pastoral letter. We ask that you heed the opportunities that are ours today. Let us not deprive the Church of the rich gifts that God has granted us.

For this reason we write to you, brothers and sisters, in the many parishes across our country. We urge the Black people of these parishes to take to heart our words of encouragement to spread the message of Christ to our own and to those of all other ethnic and racial groups. We ask pastors, co-pastors, pastoral assistants, classroom teachers and directors of religious education—indeed all who are staff and board members in the parish and in the diocese—to speak the Good News clearly in the idiom and expression of our people. Let it be the responsibility of every parish council and every parish team to ponder the meaning of Black evangelization and the burden of this pastoral letter in each respective community.

We write to those among us who are writers and poets,

---

*3-5, 41-46, 68-69, 70-73, 78-79

teachers and musicians, social scientists and theologians, philosophers and artists, academics and scholars—to all those who are the specialists whom we need to write the commentaries, edit the texts, lay out the critiques, analyze the possibilities, draw up the study guides and gather the bibliographies—to make our efforts for Black evangelization bear fruit in practical planning and innovative, imaginative proposals.

We turn to those of you who are lay leaders in the Black Catholic community. In a particular way it will be your ministry to help implement the actions called for in this letter—some on the diocesan level, others on the national level. We address the National Association of Black Catholic Administrators, the National Office of Black Catholics, and the National Black Lay Catholic Caucus. You, and those whom you represent, will be the key to unlock the doors of opportunities for a wider field of evangelization in our community.

We ask especially our brothers and sisters in the priesthood, the diaconate and the religious life, and our sisters in the consecrated life, as well as our seminarians, to aid us by your ministry to make actual in a concrete way what we have sought to set forth in guidelines and in suggested proposals. We ask for your experience as Black men and women of God, for your zealous support, and for your broad vision to give us counsel and to facilitate our common task in the service of our own people.

We look to those who are responsible on the diocesan level for the various offices and departments of education and evangelization, administrators, teachers, directors; we turn to seminary teachers and staff as well as leaders of formation; we ask all to study the proposals gathered here and to take to heart the concerns of the Church among the Black members of Christ's Body as set forth above.

Finally, we ask you, brothers in the episcopacy, upon whom weigh the cares of all the Churches and to whom the seamless robe of Christ's unity has been entrusted—we ask you, our brother bishops, to look carefully at the needs of those Black Catholics who reside within your care. Without your guidance and support the wealth of Black giftedness risks being lost, the abundance of our opportunities risks being squandered.

Last of all, we turn to Mary, the Mother of God and the

Mother of the African-American community. She is the Poor Woman and the Bearer of the Word, the first to believe and the first to proclaim the Word. We entrust to her powerful intercession this work within the Black community.

May our Heavenly Father perfect us, his Church, in faith and love, that we might be always and everywhere faithful witnesses to the power of the Resurrection of Our Lord Jesus Christ, through whom be all the honor and the glory in the Holy Spirit, now and forever. Amen.

Endnotes

1. Pope Paul VI, *On Evangelization in the Modern World*, #19.

2. The actual words of Pope Paul VI are the following:

   > If you are able to avoid the possible dangers of religious pluralism, the danger of making your Christian profession into a kind of local folklore, or into exclusivist racism, or into egoistic tribalism or arbitrary separatism, then you will be able to remain sincerely African even in your own interpretation of the Christian life; you will be able to formulate Catholicism in terms congenial to your own culture; you will be capable of bringing to the Catholic Church the precious and original contribution of "negritude," which she needs particularly in this historic hour.

   "To the Heart of Africa" (Address to the Bishops of the African Continent at the Closing Session of a Symposium Held in Kampala, Uganda), *The Pope Speaks*, vol.14 (1969), p.219.

3. From the prayer attributed to St. Francis of Assisi.

4. Pope John Paul II, "Be Witnesses to Christ, the Truth!" *You Are the Future, You Are the Hope: To the Young People of the World, John Paul II* (Daughters of Saint Paul, 1979), p. 105.

5. "God's Grandeur," *The Poems of Gerard Manley Hopkins*, 4th ed., W.H. Gardner and N.H. MacKenzie, ed. (Oxford University Press, 1970), p.66.

6. Pastoral Commission of S.C.E.P., *The Role of Women in Evangelization, Vatican II: More Postconciliar Documents*, Austin Flannery, O.P., gen. ed. (Northport, New York, 1982), p.327.

7. Pope Paul VI, Message to the World Council of Churches General Assembly at Nairobi, *Doing the Truth in Charity: Statements of Pope Paul VI, John Paul I, John Paul II, and the Secretariat for Promoting Christian Unity, 1964-1980* (Paulist Press, 1982), p.291.

8. Pope John Paul II, "The Ideal of Liberty, a Moving Force," *U.S.A.: The Message of Justice, Peace and Love* (Daughters of Saint Paul, 1979), p.96.

9. Pope John Paul II, *Redemptor Hominis*, #6.

10. *Ad Gentes (Decree on the Missionary Activity of the Church), Documents of the Second Vatican Council*, #21.

11. Pope Paul VI, *On Evangelization in the Modern World*, #63.

12. National Conference of Catholic Bishops, *Brothers and Sisters to Us: A Pastoral Letter on Racism*, *Quest for Justice*, J. Brian Benestad and Francis J. Butler, co-ed. (United States Catholic Conference, 1981), p.382.

13. *Ad Gentes (Decree on the Missionary Activity of the Church), Documents of the Second Vatican Council*, #15.

14. National Conference of Catholic Bishops, *The Program of Priestly Formation*, 3rd ed., #531,#534,#535.

15. *Ibid.*, #531,#533.

16. *Apostolicam Actuositatem (Decree on the Apostolate of the Laity), Documents of the Second Vatican Council*, #3.

17. *Ibid.*, #24.

18. "Proceedings of the First Colored Catholic Congress Held in Washington, D.C., January 1, 2 and 3, 1889," *Three Catholic Afro-American Congresses*, reprint ed. (New York, 1978), pp. 68-69.

19. *Sacrosanctum Concilium (Constitution on the Sacred Liturgy), Documents of the Second Vatican Council*, #37.

20. Pope Paul VI, *On Evangelization in the Modern World*, #47.

Most Reverend Joseph L. Howze, D.D.
    Ordained Titular Bishop of Maxita
    and Auxiliary Bishop of Natchez-Jackson,
    January 28, 1973.
    Installed Bishop of Biloxi,
    June 7, 1977.

Most Reverend Harold R. Perry, S.V.D., D.D.
    Ordained Titular Bishop of Mons in Mauretania
    and Auxiliary Bishop of New Orleans,
    January 6, 1966.

Most Reverend Eugene A. Marino, S.S.J., D.D.
    Ordained Titular Bishop of Walla Walla
    and Auxiliary Bishop of Washington, D.C.,
    July 16, 1974.

Most Reverend Joseph A. Francis, S.V.D., D.D.
    Ordained Titular Bishop of Valliposita
    and Auxiliary Bishop of Newark,
    June 25, 1976.

Most Reverend James P. Lyke, O.F.M., Ph.D.
    Ordained Titular Bishop of Fornos Maggiore
    and Auxiliary Bishop of Cleveland,
    August 1, 1979.

Most Reverend Emerson J. Moore, D.D.
    Ordained Titular Bishop of Carubi
    and Auxiliary Bishop of New York,
    September 8, 1982.

Most Reverend Moses B. Anderson, S.S.E., D.D.
    Ordained Titular Bishop of Vatarba
    and Auxiliary Bishop of Detroit
    January 27, 1983.

Most Reverend Wilton D. Gregory, D.S.L.
Ordained Titular Bishop of Oliva
and Auxiliary Bishop of Chicago,
December 13, 1983.

Most Reverend J. Terry Steib, S.V.D., D.D.
Ordained Titular Bishop of Fallaba
and Auxiliary Bishop of St. Louis,
February 10, 1984.

Most Reverend John H. Ricard, S.S.J., Ph.D. cand.
Ordained Titular Bishop of Rucuma
and Auxiliary Bishop of Baltimore,
July 2, 1984.

St. Anthony Messenger Press
1615 Republic Street, Cincinnati, Ohio 45210

$1.95